A WOMAN
of CREATIVITY

6 studies for individuals
or groups

Sandy Lar___

With Guidelines for Leaders
and Study Notes

 Women of Character Bible Studies

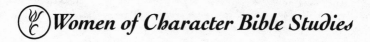

IVP

InterVarsity Press
Downers Grove, Illinois
Leicester, England

InterVarsity Press
P. O. Box 1400, Downers Grove, IL 60515, USA
38 De Montfort Street, Leicester LE1 7GP, England

©1997 by Sandy Larsen

*All rights reserved. No part of this book may be reproduced in any form without written permission from
InterVarsity Press, P.O. Box 1400, Downers Grove, IL 60515, or Inter-Varsity Press, 38 De Montfort
Street, Leicester LE1 7GP, UK.*

*InterVarsity Press® is the book-publishing division of InterVarsity Christian Fellowship®, a student
movement active on campus at hundreds of universities, colleges and schools of nursing in the United
States of America, and a member movement of the International Fellowship of Evangelical Students.
For information about local and regional activities, write Public Relations Dept., InterVarsity Christian
Fellowship, 6400 Schroeder Rd., P.O. Box 7895, Madison, WI 53707-7895.*

*Inter-Varsity Press, UK, is the book-publishing division of the Universities and Colleges Christian
Fellowship (formerly the Inter-Varsity Fellowship), a student movement linking Christian Unions in
universities and colleges throughout the United Kingdom and the Republic of Ireland, and a member
movement of the International Fellowship of Evangelical Students. For information about local and
national activities write to UCCF, 38 De Montfort Street, Leicester LE1 7GP.*

*All Scripture quotations, unless otherwise indicated, are taken from the HOLY BIBLE, NEW INTER-
NATIONAL VERSION®. NIV®. Copyright ©1973, 1978, 1984 by International Bible Society. Used
by permission of Zondervan Publishing House and Hodder and Stoughton Ltd. All rights reserved.*

Cover illustration: Claude Monet, Still Life with Apples and Grapes, *1880, oil on canvas, 66.2 ×
82.3 cm, Mr. and Mrs. Martin A. Ryerson Collection, 1933. 1157, photograph © 1996 The Art
Institute of Chicago. All rights reserved.*

USA ISBN 0-8308-2045-0

Printed in the United States of America

Contents

Cast of Characters

Setting the Stage

Each study's introduction is part of a continuing story which introduces the theme of each study. Below are the characters who play a part in the introductions.

Jeannie Rinaldo—a young single woman, who has recently graduated from community college. She has taken her first full-time job as receptionist in a busy office and just moved into her first apartment.

Will—older coworker of Jeannie

Ann—Jeannie's next-door neighbor

Gary—Ann's boyfriend

Curt—evangelism committee chair at Jeannie's church

Introducing *A Woman of Creativity*

Creativity. Does that word excite you? Or does it intimidate you?

Some of us insist we are not very creative. We deflate when confronted with Martha Stewart's pizzazzy entertaining, Margaret Mitchell's ability to write the great American novel, even our neighbor's flower arrangements. Asked to come up with a fresh idea for a church ministry or community event, we protest, "Don't ask me! I couldn't have an original idea if I tried."

Others of us have the opposite problem. We know we're creative and chafe at our lack of opportunity to express ourselves. We'd love to make stained-glass lamps and plan elaborate dinner parties, but we have no time. It's all we can do to make peanut butter sandwiches for the kids' lunch boxes and get ourselves off to work. We keep promising ourselves that "someday . . ."

Whether or not we think of ourselves as creative, the "someday" for our creativity is right now. God our Creator gives all of us the gift of originating something unique, something which no one else could make.

Some creations are tangible:

☐ a sculpture

☐ a garden

☐ a business

☐ a quilt

☐ a church ministry

Other creations are equally dynamic but less tangible:

☐ an influence for good in another person's life

☐ an unusually welcoming mood in our homes

☐ an imaginative solution to a problem

☐ a once-in-a-lifetime combining of people and re-sources to meet a particular need

Technically, we human beings do not create anything. To create as God created is to make something out of nothing, and we can't do that. Even children are conceived from the union of cells, and ideas are born in gray matter. But by God's Spirit we humans can bring about things which are new, things which would not be here if we had not cooperated with God.

In these six Scripture passages we will meet biblical people who dealt with their life situations in creative ways. We will see the Lord's creative hand at work in the details of life. And we will be encouraged to release the creative energy which God puts into our minds and our hearts. The more we release it, the more it will be renewed, because our God has no limit to his creativity.

Suggestions for Individual Study

1. As you begin each study pray that God will speak to you through his Word.

2. Read the introduction to the study, "Setting the Stage," and respond to the questions that follow it. The story is designed to draw you into the topic at hand and help you begin to see how the Scripture relates to daily life. If there will be a week or more between your studies, then you may want to read all of the introductions in one sitting to get the flow of the ongoing story. This will help if you find that you are having trouble keeping track of all the characters.

3. This is an inductive Bible study, designed to help you discover for yourself what Scripture is saying. Each study deals with a particular passage—so that you can really delve into the author's meaning in that context. Read and reread the passage to be studied. The questions are written using the language of the New International Version, so you may wish to use that version of the Bible. The New Revised Standard Version is also recommended.

4. "God's Word for Us" includes three types of questions. *Observation* questions ask about the basic facts: who, what, when, where and how. *Interpretation* questions delve into the meaning of the passage. *Application* questions (also found in the "Now or Later" section) help you discover the implications of the text for growing in Christ. These three keys unlock the treasures of Scripture.

Write your answers to the study questions in the spaces provided or in a personal journal. Writing can bring clarity and deeper understanding of yourself and of God's Word.

5. Use the study notes at the back of the guide to gain additional insight and information after you have worked through the questions for yourself.

6. Move to the "Now or Later" section. These are ideas for you to freely use in closing your study and responding to God. You may want to choose one of these to do right away and continue working through the other ideas on subsequent days to reinforce what you are learning.

Suggestions for Members of a Group Study

1. Come to the study prepared. Follow the suggestions for individual study mentioned above. You will find that careful preparation will greatly enrich your time spent in group discussion.

2. Be willing to participate in the discussion. The leader of your group will not be lecturing. Instead, she will be encouraging the members of the group to discuss what they have learned. The leader will be asking the questions that are found in this guide.

3. Stick to the topic being discussed. Your answers should be based on the verses which are the focus of the discussion and not on outside authorities such as commentaries or speakers. These studies focus on a particular passage of Scripture. Only rarely should you refer to other portions of the Bible. This allows for everyone to participate on equal ground and for in-depth study.

4. Be sensitive to the other members of the group. Listen attentively when they describe what they have learned. You may be surprised by their insights! Each question assumes a variety of answers. Many questions do not have "right" answers, particularly questions that aim at meaning or application. Instead the questions push us to explore the passage more thoroughly.

When possible, link what you say to the comments of others. Also, be affirming whenever you can. This will encourage some of the more hesitant members of the group to participate.

5. Be careful not to dominate the discussion. We are sometimes so eager to express our thoughts that we leave too little opportunity for others to respond. By all means participate! But allow others to also.

6. Expect God to teach you through the passage being discussed and through the other members of the group. Pray that you will have an enjoyable and profitable time together, but also that as a result of the study, you will find ways that you can take action individually and/or as a group.

7. It will be helpful for groups to follow a few basic guidelines. These guidelines, which you may wish to adapt to your situation, should be read at the beginning of the first session.

☐ Anything said in the group is considered confidential and will not be discussed outside the group unless specific permission is given to do so.

☐ We will provide time for each person present to talk if he or she feels comfortable doing so.

☐ We will talk about ourselves and our own situations, avoiding conversation about other people.

☐ We will listen attentively to each other.

☐ We will be very cautious about giving advice.

☐ We will pray for each other.

8. If you are the group leader, you will find additional suggestions at the back of the guide.

1

Creating Beauty

God in Our
Living Spaces

Psalm 104

 SETTING THE STAGE

"Okay, if the settee goes there under the front window, where can I put the chair?"

All weekend Jeannie Rinaldo has been busy unpacking and arranging things in her new apartment. It's actually one side of the downstairs of a rundown house converted into a triplex. Jeannie doesn't have much stuff to arrange. Besides her own bed and some furniture that didn't fit in her parents' new place, she has picked up some dishes and other kitchen things.

During community college and her first year on the job, Jeannie lived at home in the comfortable house where she grew up. Then her parents began to talk wistfully about early retirement and getting a smaller place. Jeannie prayed for guidance and got her answer: it was time to get a place of her own. And here she is, all moved in. Sure, it's different from where she grew up, but it's home.

On Monday morning the apartment seems very different to Jeannie. It smells odd. Unfamiliar. Stale. The shower is cruddy. The entire place is cramped — small living room, smaller bedroom, tiny kitchen, miniature bath. It's hard to say when the last painting and wallpapering were done, but it was years ago by someone with bad taste. The carpeting is worn thin and stained. The stove and refrigerator are old, and the previous tenant didn't leave them clean. The more Jeannie looks around, the worse it looks.

"Lord, why did you put me in this dump?" becomes Jeannie's first waking thought, sometimes expressed out loud. Each day, whether she glares resentfully at the apartment's shoddy details or goes from room to room with tunnel vision, she's just putting up with the place. She isn't really living there.

One morning as she leaves for work, Jeannie notices some straggly roses trying to bloom by the front steps. She feels a fresh stab of resentment at the landlord and life in general. Why hasn't somebody been taking care of those flowers?

Then she stops halfway down the steps. There's something touching about the bravery of those roses, blooming in spite of neglect. Jeannie hurries back into the apartment for a pair of scissors, snips off a few buds and puts them in a glass of water on her kitchen table. That evening when she comes in, the buds have gently opened to greet her. The dim little kitchen is brighter.

Plants! That's what this lifeless place needs. Jeannie knows nothing about plants, but now she wants to learn. She asks some friends at work, and they start giving her cuttings. She sticks the stems in water, sticks them into dirt when they start showing roots. Soon the place is full of greenery. Even the air is fresher when Jeannie walks in after a long workday.

She looks around and sees details differently. That stove could be clean enough if she just scrubbed at it. And that hole in the wall—why not hang a picture over it? Looking around for places to hang pictures, Jeannie notices the fine old woodwork that graced this home when it was one household and not three. Maybe it could be cleaned up. Maybe *she* could clean it up.

Who knows? Maybe this place could even be made beautiful!

1. How is Jeannie Rinaldo affected by her surroundings?

2. When you have lived in or stayed in a place that had little beauty, how did you handle it?

 GOD'S WORD FOR US
Read Psalm 104

3. Look at verses 1-9. How is the Lord pictured as actively involved in his creation? (Search for and consider especially the verbs.)

4. Water is an everyday part of our lives that we easily take for granted. How does the Lord provide for his creation through the seemingly ordinary gift of water (vv. 10-16)?

5. Humanity is introduced into this psalm in verses 14 and 15. What is the connection between human work and God's blessings? (See also v. 23.)

6. What do you learn about God from the homes he provides for his creatures (vv. 12, 17-18, 25-26)?

7. How is God showing his care for you in your physical surroundings?

8. The night activities of animals are described in verses 19-22, in contrast to the "day labor" of humans (v. 23). Night has different connotations for different people:

danger, peace, mystery. In your experience, what are some of the beauties and blessings of night?

---

9. According to verses 27-30, nature knows that it depends on God for food. When have you been most sharply aware that you are completely dependent on God for your food?

---

10. The psalmist expresses the hope—even a prayer—that the Lord will rejoice in his works (v. 31). You are one of God's works. How can your life help fulfill the psalmist's prayer?

---

11. Taking this psalm as a whole, what difference does it make to think of the world as carefully made by God?

 NOW OR LATER

Ideas to close your group meeting or personal study or for continued daily reflection.

☐ Look around your yard, a park, or another natural area for evidence of God's creative hand. Focus on small details as well as the area as a whole. How do you see God's creativity in small plant life?

trees?

insects?

birds?

soil?

the sky?

other aspects of nature?

How has human creativity teamed up with God's creativity to make things which are pleasant to look at and use? (For example: a swing set, a bench, a flower bed.)

□ Look around your home. What evidence do you see there of God's creativity and order? (Maybe all you see is *dis*order! For now don't worry about the clutter. You may even look at it as a sign of a creative mind!)

Since most things in your home are probably made by people, where do you see the teamwork of divine and human creativity?

As you look around for evidence of God's creativity, don't overlook the people—yourself and others!

□ For further study read Genesis 1—2. Consider how each additional aspect of God's creation added to the whole and graced what God had made before.

2

....

Drudgery
or Discovery?
Christ in the
Daily Grind

John 4:1-26

 SETTING THE STAGE

"There's a call for you on line 4."

"Just a moment, I'll see if he's in."

"I'm sorry, she's out of the office now, would you like her voice mail?"

As she hangs up the phone and turns back to her keyboard, Jeannie Rinaldo wonders, *How many times a day do I say the same thing?*

At first Jeannie was excited about her job as receptionist in a busy office. There was always something going on. Now she's realizing it's always the same old somethings going on. This afternoon she's especially feeling the tedium. She tells herself, *I could easily be replaced by a computer with a nice voice.*

Visitors come through the door with that same tentative look on their faces and ask the same questions. The stuff she types is the routine boring overflow from the other secretaries. She can tell which extensions will be answered instantly and which ones will ring forever. Her coworkers make the same stale remarks as they hurry past.

Her teeth go on edge as Will comes in after lunch. He's worked there forever, and she knows he'll make the same old joke: "Did the President call me back yet?"

What's that? Did Will go by without saying a word? Good! Jeannie turns to her keyboard. In a few minutes Will gets a phone call, and when she rings his extension, he answers instantly. Very unusual.

Soon Will is on his way out again. He looks like he's in a fog. Something isn't right. Jeannie hears herself say, "Will! If the President calls, should I take a message?"

Will stares at Jeannie like he's trying to remember who she is. Finally he answers, "Hold my calls, will you? I have to go back to the hospital."

"Hospital? Why?" It's not a polite question, but she can't ignore Will's obvious distress.

"It's our little granddaughter. She was born at midnight last night, but she's having some problems . . ." His voice catches and he starts to turn away.

"I'm really sorry to hear that." Jeannie feels she should say more. "Do you mind if I pray for her? I mean—and for your whole family too?" *Uh-oh! What if I get in trouble for asking that?*

Will looks surprised but not offended. "Thanks, Jeannie. We'd appreciate that." He manages a slight smile before he turns to leave.

Jeannie sits and lets the incident sink in. Even when the phone summons her back to work, she continues to pray for Will's granddaughter and to think about what just happened. She hadn't even known that Will had a grandchild on the way. *Lord, is this a message from you? How much do I really know about the people I work with every day?*

1. What made the difference in transforming Jeannie's day from monotonous to meaningful?

2. In your experience, what has given meaning to monotonous tasks?

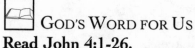 GOD'S WORD FOR US
Read John 4:1-26.

3. What do verses 1-8 tell us about what Jesus might have been thinking and feeling?

4. Look at verses 6-10. What do we know about the woman's situation?

5. When the woman heard Jesus' promise of living water, what were her reactions (vv. 10-15)?

6. What was she beginning to plan and hope for (v. 15)?

7. When have you wished you could call a halt and resign from all your work? (Consider your job, motherhood, household chores, volunteer work and so on.)

8. How did Jesus surprise the woman in the midst of their conversation about water (vv. 16-18)?

9. As you go about your daily work, what wrong attitudes and actions might be weighing you down and adding to your sense of drudgery?

10. The woman tried to involve Jesus in the old contro-versy of the right place to worship (v. 19). Refusing to be sidetracked, what did Jesus tell her about true worship (vv. 21-24)?

11. When we have a challenging job to do, it's natural to reach out to the Lord in prayer. Why is it harder to think of Christ when we're engaged in ordinary tasks?

12. How can you be more sensitive to the presence of Christ in your daily work?

 NOW OR LATER

☐ When the Samaritan woman came to the well, she was not looking for a spiritual experience. Certainly she did not expect to meet the Messiah. To this burdened person doing chores in the noonday heat, Jesus chose to reveal himself. At any time she could have filled her water jar and left, but she stayed because she was open to his revelation. When have you unexpectedly experienced Christ in the midst of mundane tasks? Maybe it happened in ways like these:

You encountered a needy person in the laundromat or grocery store and took time to listen. Afterward you remembered that "whatever you did for one of the least of these brothers of mine, you did for me" (Matthew 25:40).

You were irritated at something — a computer program, your car, a salesperson, a traffic light — and you prayed and experienced God's peace in spite of the frustration.

In your annoyance at drudge jobs, the Holy Spirit exposed a nerve. Gently he showed you some attitude such as pride or discontent which you needed to confess and change. You experienced Christ's forgiveness and renewal.

You resolved to do the most mundane task as service to the Lord (Colossians 3:23), and your attitude toward that job was transformed.

□ Yow will you plan this week to be open to discovering Christ in the daily grind of housework?
family responsibilities?
your job?
bothersome people you have to see frequently?
repetitive tasks?

□ For further study read the rest of John 4. It tells the further results of the Samaritan woman's encounter with Jesus. It's not only for the sake of relieving our own boredom that we should stay open to meeting Christ in our everyday tasks. When we encounter him and are transformed by him, others will benefit.

3

....

A Gift at the Right Time
Inventive Caring

1 Samuel 25:2-35

 ## SETTING THE STAGE

As Jeannie Rinaldo comes home to her plant-filled and freshly painted apartment, she's singing a little song of praise to God. Today Will reported that his baby grand-daughter has turned the corner and should be going home tomorrow. Jeannie's job has become much more interesting. Making the effort to really get to know the people at work has made all the difference.

The evening ahead doesn't look bleak, though Jeannie expects to spend it alone, because she's learning to make bread and has a new recipe to experiment with. She enjoys the gratifying feel of kneading the dough. Maybe she'll plan a party for next week and invite some of the young single people from work—now that she's not so ashamed of where she lives.

There's still one embarrassing thing about living here. And just as Jeannie puts the loaves in the oven to bake, that embarrassment rings the bell. It's Ann, the woman who lives in the other downstairs apartment. They don't talk much, except that Ann is always asking Jeannie for some little favor or other.

Ann's home is in as much disarray as the rest of her existence. She sits on her cluttered steps for hours talking on her cordless phone. She has two small children plus a new boyfriend, Gary, who recently took up residence in Ann's life and in her apartment.

Now Ann is at the door saying, "Hey, Jeannie, can I use your phone?" She's made the same request the past several evenings. "Uh—sure, I guess so, Ann. Is yours not working?"

"Gary didn't pay the bill, so they cut us off. They're not supposed to do that. Can you watch my kids while I make one quick call?"

Ann comes in Jeannie's front door, and Jeannie goes out and then into Ann's front door, where she finds the two kids sprawled on the floor in front of a big TV. There's a garbagey smell in the air. Carefully Jeannie sits on the least dirty spot on the couch and tries to talk with the kids, but she can't pry their attention from the screen.

Then with no warning the five-year-old says, "Gary's not coming back."

Jeannie isn't sure what to say. Do the kids think of their mother's boyfriend as their dad? As a visitor? Living next to Ann has shown Jeannie what a sheltered life she led before she left home.

Ann is back—and angry. "I called where he works, and they said he doesn't work there anymore! They're lying! I called his brother, and he says he's out of town. Then I called the phone company. They're supposed to call me back, so I gave them your number. Gee, your kitchen smells good. What are you making?"

Just one quick call, huh? "Bread," Jeannie answers curtly.

"I wish I knew how to do that," Ann says as Jeannie leaves, feeling used and manipulated. So she's been giving Ann the benefits of a free phone while Ann ignores an unpaid bill! *Lord, why did you put me next door to such a needy person?*

Her own prayer haunts her. Certainly the Lord, not chance, put her next door to Ann. But what does Ann actually need? Her problems are so complicated.

The buzzer on the oven timer startles Jeannie. Time to take the loaves out of the oven. All day she's been looking forward to peanut butter melted into fresh, hot, home-made bread. She shakes the loaves out of their pans, and it's as though a voice in her head says, *Take that over to Ann. Both loaves.*

"Lord, are you kidding?" Jeannie responds out loud. "I've been looking forward to this all day! Besides, she doesn't need bread. She needs a whole new lifestyle."

Of course she does. So take that bread over to Ann and then offer to teach her how to make it herself.

"But she's an irresponsible freeloader!"

You're right, she is. It's all she knows how to be. And you can start to show her a whole different lifestyle. Start by taking an interest and teaching her something wholesome and good.

Yes, Jeannie has to admit, *that might be good for Ann.* She takes a final wistful sniff and goes out the door with both loaves of bread and a copy of the recipe.

———

1. How is creativity bringing wholeness to Jeannie's life?

How might Jeannie be able to help Ann in practical ways while still helping her take responsibility for her life?

 GOD'S WORD FOR US

Read 1 Samuel 25:2-35.

Background: After escaping from his master, King Saul, who had tried to kill him, David was living as an outcast in the wilderness. With the skill of a military leader he kept moving to different strongholds accompanied by several hundred men who had given him loyalty. Nabal had grazed sheep in the area where David was hiding out, and David, once a shepherd boy himself, had protected Nabal's flocks and shepherds.

---

2. Describe the contrast between Abigail and her husband Nabal (vv. 2-3).

---

3. What conflict was set up by David's request of Nabal (vv. 4-13)?

---

4. Why was Abigail a good person to enlist for help (vv. 14-17)?

5. The servant told Abigail, "Now think it over and see what you can do" (v. 17). Why is that excellent advice for anyone wishing to intervene to help someone else?

6. How did Abigail show initiative in responding to the emergency (vv. 18-19)?

7. When have you wanted to intervene and offer help but been afraid to take the risk?

8. What might David have thought and felt as he met Abigail and her caravan and realized what she was doing (vv. 20-22)?

9. How did Abigail's words meet David's needs even more deeply than her gifts of food (vv. 23-31)?

10. What do verses 32-35 reveal about David's reaction to the unexpected encounter?

11. When have someone's unexpected gift and/or words to you made a crucial difference in your life?

12. What aspects of this story give you courage to offer help?

 NOW OR LATER

☐ "I'd like to help So-and-So, but I don't know how." Often we sincerely want to help, but we draw a blank on the practical specifics of what to do. The advice the servant gave Abigail is good advice for us: "Now think it over." Take the need out of the realm of the vague and general. Focus your mind and heart, and reflect on as many specific details about the need as you can.

Consider the particular personalities and idiosyncrasies of the people involved.

Consider time factors.

Think through cautions you should take so your help won't backfire.

What are the deeper needs beneath the obvious surface ones?

Next, "see what you can do." Think about what *you* can uniquely do to help, taking into account your gifts and talents.

How well do you know the people involved?

Who else do you know who could be tapped to help?

How can you keep from duplicating what others are doing?

How do finances factor in?

time constraints?

Remember that people's spiritual needs are bound up in their physical and emotional needs. Any plan for physical help can become an avenue for spiritual help.

☐ For further study from the perspective of the recipient of a generous gift, read Philippians 4:10-19, Paul's thank-you for a gift of love received at the right time.

4

....

I Insist
on It
Hospitality

Acts 16:11-15, 40

 SETTING THE STAGE

After church Sunday morning, Jeannie is approached by
Curt, who heads up the evangelism committee. From his
first words he's clearly a man making a sales pitch. "Jeannie! Did you know the church is planning a summer
outreach to underprivileged kids?"

"No, I didn't know that. That sounds good."

"You know we have a lot of kids here for Bible school,
but we've never succeeded in bringing in the ones from
the poorer neighborhoods, and we figure it's about time
we tried something different."

"Uh-huh." Jeannie isn't sure why Curt is bringing this
up with her. She has no particular gift for working with
children.

"It'll be for five days, early evenings, so it's after work.
It's a great program. We'll play games at Mitchell Park
and then have a Bible story. For the Bible story we'll split
them up by ages, and first we'll have refreshments . . ."

"Mitchell Park? That's only a block from my house. You mean it's in my neighborhood?"

"Sure." Curt obviously doesn't realize that Jeannie has a hard time thinking of herself as living in a poor neighborhood! He gets to the heart of the matter by stating, "We'd love to have you be part of it. Think you can help out?"

"Me?" Her first impulse is to say no. She taught Bible school one summer while she was at the community college, but she wasn't comfortable doing it and no one begged her to come back. "Really, I'm not all that great with kids. I'm definitely not a teacher, and I'm no good at organizing games." She can see that Curt has heard this story before. "I suppose you're having trouble getting people to volunteer, huh?"

Curt's cheerful demeanor falls away. "To tell the truth, yes. Everybody's so busy, and it's not the sort of thing people are lining up to do. It's not very . . ."

"Glamorous?"

"Right."

Jeannie understands. It didn't feel very glamorous when she took that bread over to Ann's unappealing apartment. But the fresh, honest bread was like incense from another world for Ann. It started the two women talking, and in continued conversations Ann has opened up about her life.

Now here comes something else new. Jeannie knows that lately God has been pushing her beyond her comfort zone, both at work and at home, showing her different ways of doing things. She could at least take Ann's kids to this outreach at the park. She asks, "My neighbor has a five-year-old and a six-year-old. How many kids that age do you think there'll be?"

"Not many," Curt assures her quickly, like a man sensing a sale. "It isn't like there are lots of apartments in that area. It's mostly those duplexes and triplexes. You live in one of those, don't you?"

Jeannie thinks of her triplex with its oversized porch, its large overgrown backyard. Suddenly she sees the porch and yard full of neighborhood kids. No way! They'd be coming in to use the bathroom, picking up anything that looked interesting, maybe stealing. But if they were well supervised and she set limits—well, her home is something unique that she can offer.

"Curt, what if you brought the younger kids over to my house for refreshments and the Bible story? I'd have to have certain rules, of course, but we could use the yard and the porch. Then they'd know that somebody from the church lives right in the neighborhood. Would that help?"

"Would that help!" Curt looks as though Jeannie has just saved his neck. She only hopes she hasn't stuck her own neck out too far.

---

1. What risks is Jeannie taking by inviting the neighborhood kids over?

---

2. What experiences have you had with offering your home for ministry?

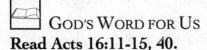 GOD'S WORD FOR US
Read Acts 16:11-15, 40.
Background: "We" (vv. 11-12) includes Paul, Silas, Timo-

thy and Luke. They traveled to Macedonia because Paul had seen a vision which he took as a call to preach the gospel there (Acts 16:9-10).

3. How was Lydia's heart already prepared to be opened to the gospel (vv. 13, 14)?

4. How did Lydia respond to the gospel (v. 15)?

5. What practical help did she offer the apostles (v. 15)?

6. When (if ever) does it feel natural for you to offer help like this?

7. Verses 16-39 relate how Paul and Silas were arrested, cruelly treated and put into prison. An earthquake could have freed them, but they stayed, and the jailer and his family were converted to Christ. The next morning they were released when it was discovered that they were Roman citizens. What do their actions in verse 40 show about their priorities?

---

8. What does verse 40 reveal about Lydia?

---

9. Beginning at the riverside when Lydia became a Christian believer, what risks was she taking with her offer of hospitality?

---

10. How does hospitality inconvenience the one who offers it?

---

11. How does hospitality bless the one who offers it?

 NOW OR LATER

☐ When has someone made you feel really comfortable in their home? Journal about your experience. Include specific actions of the host and aspects of the environment that made you feel at home.

☐ As a prosperous businesswoman, Lydia probably had a spacious and well-appointed home. Your home may not live up to that standard. The size of a home may dictate the number of people you can accommodate, but they have little to do with how welcoming your home is.

Spend some time brainstorming about ways you could extend hospitality. You're not making any commitments, you're just coming up with ideas! How could you use your home for ministry to individuals in the church?

individuals outside the church?

groups in the church?

groups outside the church?

If you feel reluctant to invite people into your home, what are the obstacles? How can some be overcome? (For example, how can you creatively "host" them in a park, a fast food place or a coffee shop?)

☐ Perhaps you are concerned about the risks associated with hospitality. While it's impossible to eliminate all risks, consider ways to manage them. For example, try
making parts of your home off-limits.
setting realistic limits on length and frequency of visits.
explaining limitations in advance, such as whether small children are welcome.

☐ For further study read Luke 24:13-35, in which two followers of Jesus were blessed when they offered him hospitality before they even realized who he was.

5

....

Give Us Ten Days
Imaginative Problem-Solving

Daniel 1:1-21

 SETTING THE STAGE

"What do you mean you can't do it?" Will is amazed at Jeannie. "It isn't just anybody they're having take this training. Obviously you're being groomed to move up."

Jeannie has already advanced in her work and now supervises several other people in the office. As the challenges of her job increase, she has to keep relying on the Lord for creative solutions to problems. It's been good for her mental powers and for her spiritual growth.

She answers, "I'd prefer not to take the training, Will. I've heard a lot about this program. It isn't just management techniques. It also has a spiritual emphasis."

"So? What's wrong with that? I'd think that would be right up your alley." Jeannie has had Will's respect since that day she prayed for his granddaughter.

"Yes and no. There are some spiritual things that, as a Christian, I just can't go along with. For instance, they have you visualize your perfect inner self, right? And they tell you to go to that inner self for all your answers. I don't believe in that."

Will leans back in his chair. "Sounds like you've done some homework on this."

"Well, there are some of us at my church who like to keep up on"—how should she put it? Keep up on New Age thinking?—"on what you might call religious ideas in business and medicine and so forth. One of the things we looked into was management training courses. This is one I just can't take with a clear conscience."

"Look, Jeannie, it's fine to have convictions about things, but around here you have to keep them to yourself. They're telling you to take this course. If you're going to be a team player, you can't say no." Will leans forward and says with intensity, "They've got their eye on you. You're brighter than anybody else around here, and they know it. But you start letting your beliefs interfere with your work, and they'll change their minds about you real fast. Take my advice. Take the training and keep your mouth shut."

Jeannie's stomach is churning as she goes back to her desk. She appreciates Will's concern, but he doesn't understand her conflict. She can't give the management people what they want.

Wait a minute. What do the management people want? Productivity. Initiative. Imaginative solutions to problems. They also want team players—no free spirits.

Sucking in a deep breath, Jeannie starts composing a memo to the members of the management team:

I deeply appreciate being chosen to take the upcoming personal-effectiveness training. For personal reasons I wish to propose an alternative training and goal-setting for myself which will harmonize well with our team goals. With your approval I will

complete—on my own—a time-management workshop and
will set a series of higher productivity goals for the next six
months. At that time I will be happy to meet with you and
review my progress. Thank you for your understanding.

Jeannie Rinaldo

---

1. What does Jeannie hope to achieve by her alternative
plan?

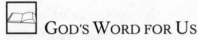 GOD'S WORD FOR US
Read Daniel 1:1-21.

---

2. How had the Jews been made subservient to Babylon
(vv. 1-2)?

---

3. Why were Daniel and the other three young Israelites
selected for special training (vv. 3-7)?

---

4. What was the conflict which Daniel faced between the
Babylonian regime and his religion (v. 8)?

5. Why did the official think it was impossible to accommodate Daniel's conscience (vv. 9-10)?

6. What dilemma are you facing now in which you feel caught between two possibilities, neither of which seems good?

7. What solution did Daniel suggest to the chief official (vv. 11-14)?

8. Faced with a dilemma where there seems to be no good solution, do you tend to search for other possibilities or do you go with the flow?

9. What was the outcome of Daniel's alternative solution (vv. 15-16)?

10. How was God directly involved in helping the four Israelites make a good impression on the Babylonians (vv. 17-20)?

11. Why was Daniel's idea a good solution for the king?

the chief official?

the four young Israelites?

12. What help do you need from God and/or from others to solve dilemmas you are facing?

 NOW OR LATER

☐ In your journal, jot down some problems in the past where God provided an unexpected answer. Write your thoughts about recalling God's surprises. How do they help give you confidence for present and future dilemmas?

☐ When we're caught between two apparently bad choices, God will often give us a third alternative if we look for it. Brainstorm some alternative solutions to a dilemma you face now: a third way to solve the problem, a fourth way, a fifth way and so forth. (If you are in a group, brainstorm possibilities for each other's problems. But leave to each person the final choice of what to do.)

☐ The fact that we can think of a creative solution to a problem doesn't mean it's the right thing to do. Bring each possible solution to the Lord in prayer. Ask which one you should choose, and pray that you'll be open to still other creative solutions as God guides you.

☐ For further study read John 8:1-11. Here Jesus is faced with a situation where he apparently can't win, and he gives a powerful, unexpected answer.

6

....

Never Too Late
Taking Initiative

Ruth 2:1-12

 SETTING THE STAGE

Sunday afternoon. Jeannie Rinaldo stands in the door-way between her kitchen and living room, surveying her small apartment. It's barely recognizable from the gloomy place she moved into. Fresh paint, wallpaper borders, colorful knickknacks here and there. She's especially proud of a small table she refinished herself, where she displays her favorite plant, a delicate spreading fern.

Plants are thriving all over the apartment in attractive pots. *They're like symbols of my own growth,* she thinks. *My spiritual life since I left home has flourished like these plants.*

Today, like the day she moved in, there are packing boxes scattered around the house. This time they're for moving out. With her increase in salary, Jeannie is on her way to a nicer apartment. But there is something about this place she will always cherish.

She'll be back in the neighborhood on Sundays though.

She's been taking her neighbor's two children to Sunday school, and she plans to continue to pick them up. So far she hasn't talked Ann into coming to church with her, but she prays the time will come.

Ann comes over with a fistful of papers the kids have brought home from church. "It says here there's a day camp coming up," she says. "At a lake."

"Oh, yeah, I saw that. Are you sending them?"

"I'd like to. It sounds really good." She reads from the paper: " 'Music, crafts, Bible stories, swimming.' They've only been to a lake a few times, but they love the water. It'd be so good for them."

"So, are they going?"

Ann chews her lip. "Well, I notice it isn't free, like what you had at the park and here at your house."

"Oh. Well, yes, I suppose they have to rent the facilities and provide lunches and lifeguards and so forth."

"I can't afford it," Ann says bluntly.

Jeannie knows that's true. Ann recently paid a sizable deposit to have her phone reconnected. Once "I can't afford it" would have been followed by a shameless "Will you pay their way?" Lately Ann hasn't been asking for so much from Jeannie. Still, her statement hangs in the air and demands a response.

Jeannie wants to say, "Don't worry, I'll pay for it." But will it help this family if she just foots the bill like so many other people have done for them? On the other hand, if she doesn't pay their way, it will only deprive the kids of going to day camp.

Lord, why does life have to be full of so many questions? Especially ones that don't have easy answers? It's a prayer Jeannie has prayed often in many forms since she left home. She decides to acknowledge Ann's statement but not offer any financial help. "That's too bad," she says. "Maybe something will come up."

"Maybe, but I doubt it." Ann wads up the papers. "Can I throw these out here?"

"Just leave them on the table."

After her neighbor leaves, Jeannie scans the papers absentmindedly. Maybe she should offer to pay. Maybe she shouldn't split hairs. Hmm. Lots of stuff going on at church this week. They're always looking for people to do things. Not all the work is volunteer, of course, like this notice for extra custodial help.

Custodial help? A few hours a week? And it pays something! Jeannie hurries next door.

"Ann! Did you see this?" She practically sticks the bulletin in Ann's face. "You could do the work while the kids are at day camp, and we could arrange for a ride for them, and you could earn their camp fees!" Since Jeannie thinks it's the greatest idea since the microwave, Ann's reaction disappoints her.

"Cleaning? The last time I tried to do something like that I threw my back out and couldn't move for a week. I can't lift anything over ten pounds."

This is the first Jeannie has heard about Ann having a bad back. She wants to shoot back, "Okay, forget it."

She makes a gentler answer. "I'll talk to you again, okay?" Back home, she looks around at the place which used to be so dismal and now glows with life. When she leaves, she'll give all these plants to Ann and start over with new ones in her new place. She prays that the greenery will be as much of a life-giving boost to her neighbor as it was for her.

Meanwhile, Jeannie's mind starts whirling, searching for still another imaginative solution with God's help.

1. What are some ways Jeannie has shown initiative in solving problems?

2. How can she encourage Ann to take more initiative to help herself?

 GOD'S WORD FOR US
Read Ruth 2:1-12.
Background: In the time of the judges, before Israel had their first king, a woman named Naomi and her husband and two sons left Bethlehem because of a famine and went to live in the country of Moab on the other side of the Dead Sea. There the two sons married Moabite women. After all three men had died, Naomi decided to go home to Bethlehem. One daughter-in-law stayed in Moab, but Ruth was determined to go with Naomi, vowing that Naomi's people would be her people and Naomi's God would be her God (Ruth 1:16-18). Back in Bethlehem, in a culture in which women were economically dependent on men, the two women faced poverty.

3. What action did Ruth take to help herself and Naomi (vv. 1-3)?

4. How did Ruth impress the harvest foreman (vv. 4-7)?

5. As Ruth took action, how had God prepared her circumstances in advance (vv. 1, 3-5, 8-12)?

6. In what ways did Boaz care for and encourage Ruth (vv. 8-12)?

7. How did God's sovereignty and Ruth's initiative work together to meet her needs and Naomi's?

8. When have you seen God's sovereignty and human initiative (either your own or someone else's) working together to solve a problem?

9. "I'll wait and see what God does" can be a statement of faith. It can also be dangerous passivity. In your own experience how have you known the difference?

———————————————————————————————

10. In what situation are you being overly passive now?

———————————————————————————————

11. How will you take fresh initiative with God's help?

 NOW OR LATER

☐ There was another famine many generations before Ruth, in Jacob's time. Jacob heard there was grain in Egypt, but his grown sons took no action. They let their problem immobilize them. Finally Jacob demanded, "Why do you just keep looking at each other?" (Genesis 42:1). His sons were showing far less initiative than Ruth the Moabites!

Think about a chronically troublesome situation which makes you mope or feel helpless. What action could you take, consistent with Scripture, to change the situation for the better?

to change yourself for the better?

☐ At times, even while we're relying on the Lord, we need a push from another person to get moving. If you are studying in a group, consider: In what ways are we just "standing around looking at each other"?

How will we plan to encourage each other to follow through on actions we need to take? (For example, phone calls, "reminder" or "encouragement" notes, having a time of accountability in your meetings.)

☐ If you are doing this study on your own, consider making a mutual agreement with one other Christian who also needs to take some action. Agree to be accountable to each other and check up on each other's progress.

☐ For further study read 2 Timothy 1:1-7, where Paul encourages Timothy to go forward in faith, not shrink back in fear.

Guidelines for Leaders

My grace is sufficient for you. (2 Corinthians 12:9)

If leading a Bible study is something new for you, don't worry. These studies are designed to be led easily. As a matter of fact, the flow of questions through the passage from observation to interpretation to application is so natural that you may feel that the studies lead themselves.

You don't need to be an expert on the Bible or a trained teacher to lead a Bible discussion. The idea behind these inductive studies is that the leader guides group members to discover for themselves what the Bible has to say. This method of learning will allow group members to remember much more of what is said than a lecture would.

This study guide is flexible. You can use it with a variety of groups—student, professional, neighborhood or church groups. Each study takes about forty-five minutes in a group setting with the possibility of extending the time to sixty minutes or more by adding questions from "Now or Later."

There are some important facts to know about group dynamics and encouraging discussion. The suggestions listed below should enable you to effectively and enjoyably fulfill your role as leader.

Preparing for the Study

1. Ask God to help you understand and apply the passage in your own life. Unless this happens, you will not be prepared to lead others. Pray too for the various members of the group. Ask God to open your hearts to the message of his Word and motivate you to action.

2. Read the introduction to the entire guide to get an overview of the subject at hand and the issues which will be explored. Also read through the introductions to each study to get the flow of the continuing story that runs through the guide and to get familiar with the characters. Be ready to refer the group to the list of characters on the back of the contents page if they have questions about the story.

3. As you begin each study, read and reread the assigned Bible passage to familiarize yourself with it.

4. This study guide is based on the New International Version of the Bible. It will help you and the group if you use this translation as the basis for your study and discussion.

5. Carefully work through each question in the study. Spend time in meditation and reflection as you consider how to respond.

6. Write your thoughts and responses in the space provided in the study guide. This will help you to express your understanding of the passage clearly.

7. It might help you to have a Bible dictionary handy. Use it to look up any unfamiliar words, names or places. (For additional help on how to study a passage, see chapter five of *Leading Bible Discussions*, InterVarsity Press.)

8. Take the "Now or Later" portion of each study seriously. Consider how you need to apply the Scripture to your life. Remember that the group will follow your lead in responding to the studies. They will not go any deeper than you do.

Leading the Study

1. Begin the study on time. Open with prayer, asking God to help the group to understand and apply the passage.

2. Be sure that everyone in your group has a study guide. Encourage the group to prepare beforehand for each discussion by reading the introduction to the guide and by working through the questions in the study.

3. At the beginning of your first time together, explain that these studies are meant to be discussions, not lectures. Encourage the members of the group to participate. However, do not put pressure on those who may be hesitant to speak during the first few sessions.

4. Have a group member read the story in "Setting the Stage" at the beginning of the discussion or allow group members some time to read this silently. These stories are designed to draw the readers into the topic of the study and show how the topic is related to our daily lives. It is merely a starting point so don't allow the group members to get bogged down with details of the story or with trying to make a literal connection to the passage to be studied. Just enjoy them.

5. Every study begins with one or more "approach" questions, which are meant to be asked before the passage is read. These questions are designed to connect the opening story with the theme of the study and to encourage group members to begin to open up. Encourage as many members as possible to participate and be ready to get the discussion going with your own response.

Approach questions can reveal where our thoughts or feelings need to be transformed by Scripture. That is why it is especially important not to read the passage before the approach question is asked. The passage will tend to color the honest reactions people would otherwise give because they are, of course, supposed to think the way the Bible does.

6. Have a group member read aloud the passage to be studied.

7. As you ask the questions under "God's Word for Us," keep in mind that they are designed to be used just as they are written. You may simply read them aloud. Or you may prefer to express them in your own words.

There may be times when it is appropriate to deviate from the study guide. For example, a question may have already been answered. If so, move on to the next question. Or someone may raise an important question not covered in the guide. Take time to discuss it, but try to keep the group from going off on tangents.

8. Avoid answering your own questions. If necessary, repeat or rephrase them until they are clearly understood. An eager group quickly becomes passive and silent if they think the leader will do most of the talking.

9. Don't be afraid of silence. People may need time to think about the question before formulating their answers.

10. Don't be content with just one answer. Ask, "What do the rest of you think?" or "anything else?" until several people have given answers to the question.

11. Acknowledge all contributions. Try to be affirming whenever possible. Never reject an answer. If it is clearly off-base, ask, "Which verse led you to that conclusion?" or again, "What do the rest of you think?"

12. Don't expect every answer to be addressed to you,

even though this will probably happen at first. As group members become more at ease, they will begin to truly interact with each other. This is one sign of healthy discussion.

13. Don't be afraid of controversy. It can be very stimulating. If you don't resolve an issue completely, don't be frustrated. Move on and keep it in mind for later. A subsequent study may solve the problem.

14. Periodically summarize what the group has said about the passage. This helps to draw together the various ideas mentioned and gives continuity to the study. But don't preach.

15. "Now or Later" can be used in a variety of ways depending on the time available to you and the interests of your group members. You may want to discuss an application question or idea and make some commitments. Or you may want to allow five minutes or so of quiet reflection within the group time so that people can journal their responses. Then, ask simply, "What did you experience (and/or learn) as you journaled?"

You will want to use at least one of these ideas to wrap up the group time, but you may want to encourage group members to continue working through other ideas throughout the week. You can continue discussing what has been learned at your next meeting.

16. Conclude your time together with conversational prayer. Ask for God in following through on the commitments you've made.

17. End on time.

Many more suggestions and helps are found in *Small Group Leaders' Handbook* and *The Big Book on Small Groups* (both from InterVarsity Press). Reading through one of these books would be worth your time.

Study Notes

Study 1. Creating Beauty: God in Our Living Spaces. Psalm 104.

Purpose: To become more aware of the beauty God has put into the details of our world.

Question 3. This passage is poetic imagery expressing literal truth. God does not literally wear a garment of light or ride on the wind, but his Spirit is intimately involved in the details of the natural world.

Question 5. Group members may have differing reactions to the idea of work as a blessing from God. Those who love their jobs or who have gone through unemployment are more likely to see work as a blessing. Those whose jobs are drudgery may have trouble seeing a connection between God and work. Notice in verses 14-15 that humanity works at cultivating the plants which give us good products; we are involved in the process by which God gives us much to enjoy. Work from morning till evening is part of the rhythm of all life on earth (vv. 19-23). This psalm indicates that life would have less meaning if humanity had no work to do.

Question 6. The homes are specially designed and fitting for the various creatures. God cares for each one and provides what is needed for its welfare.

Question 7. When we think of our physical surround-ings, most of us find something to complain about. This question leads us to begin to consider our surroundings in a positive light in preparation for the activities in "Now or Later."

Question 8. Answers to this question will depending on experience and background. Rural night, city night, small-town night and suburban night have very different qualities. If group members are slow getting started, suggest they think of how they experience night through their five senses: sight, hearing, taste, touch, smell.

Question 10. Consider what pleases the Lord, and ask how and whether your life gives him reason for pleasure.

Study 2. Drudgery or Discovery? Christ in the Daily Grind. John 4:1-26.

Purpose: To keep our eyes, ears and hearts open to see Christ in our everyday chores.

Question 1. Note how Jeannie's focus turned away from the work routine and toward the human factor—the people around her, and her own response to those people.

Question 3. Jesus was experiencing the beginnings of conflict over his ministry (vv. 1-3), physical weariness from his journey (v. 6), thirst (v. 7) and hunger (v. 8). There would have been some tension in the air as he initiated a conversation with a Samaritan woman, for two reasons: the impropriety of a rabbi talking with a woman in public, and the racial conflict between Samaritans and Jews.

Question 4. Samaritans were of mixed Jewish-Gentile ancestry and were eternally at odds with the Jews. They believed in God and the Law of Moses, but they rejected

Jerusalem as their holy site and worshiped instead on Mt. Gerizim. Near Mt. Gerizim was Jacob's well, which had become the town well for the village of Sychar. Getting water from a well was a simple but laborious job of lowering an empty container and hauling it up full. Drawing and carrying water was the constant task of women in Jesus' time, as it has been the task of women all over the world.

This encounter happened at about the sixth hour from sunrise—that is, noon. The heat of midday was not the usual time to draw water. The Samaritan woman may have chosen that time to go to the well in order to avoid her neighbors who disapproved of her morals. In that case she was burdened not only with her water jar but with her conscience.

Questions 5-6. It was difficult for the woman to see beyond the promise of physical relief from daily drudgery. When we are caught up in the physical details of the daily grind, it's hard for us to shift our focus and concentrate on our spiritual lives.

Question 8. Spiritual and moral issues surprise us when they're suddenly brought up in the midst of our routine work. Perhaps that's the best place to consider them, in the middle of real life, rather than in some cloistered setting.

Study 3. A Gift at the Right Time: Inventive Caring. 1 Samuel 25:2-35.

Purpose: To motivate us to think of and carry out creative acts of caring.

Question 1. Think of ways Jeannie might help Ann accomplish things for herself and be less dependent, for example, talking about a plan to get the phone bill paid off. Jeannie also needs to decide and tell Ann the limits about phone use, babysitting and other favors.

Question 3. "Nabal resided in Maon but pastured his large flocks of sheep and goats in Carmel (now el-Kurmul) on the edge of the wilderness of Judah. As he was celebrating the shearing of his sheep, David, whose band of followers appears to have protected the flocks of Nabal from the predatory raids of the Bedouins, sent ten of his men to collect 'payment' for this service. Nabal not only categorically refused to give the messengers anything, but also grievously insulted David and his followers" (E. R. Dalglish, "Nabal," in *Interpreter's Dictionary of the Bible*, vol. 3 [Nashville, Tenn.: Abingdon Press, 1962], p. 491).

Question 4. The servant knew that Abigail knew Nabal better than anyone. Apparently he also knew she had a realistic picture of her husband and would not defend or deny his meanness.

Question 5. The servant's words call for two things: caution and action. First he told Abigail to think it over. A person who wants to help should not rush into the first course of action which comes to mind. Even in an emergency, the helper needs to weigh the situation and size up the pros and cons of different actions. Paramedics and emergency room staff take time — even if only seconds — to evaluate a patient, reject some courses of action and choose others. Next the servant told Abigail to see what she could do. Instead of wasting time considering things we can't do, we should look at what we have in our power to do. (Perhaps God will have someone else do what we can't!) While there were plenty of things Abigail could not do, such as physically restrain her husband or cancel his orders to fight, she could originate a plan for heading off David's attack.

Question 8. David was furious, feeling wronged, out to

get revenge on Nabal. The last thing he expected was to be met with generous gifts. The element of surprise and his growing curiosity would have disarmed his anger.

Question 9. Abigail validated David's opinion of Nabal (v. 25). She reminded him that the Lord had kept him from killing others for revenge (v. 26). She expressed certainty that David would have future success (vv. 28-31). She explained that she wanted to protect him from a guilty conscience (v. 31).

Study 4. I Insist on It: Hospitality. Acts 16:11-15, 40.
Purpose: To resolve to let the Lord welcome people to himself through our hospitality.

Question 3. Apparently Lydia made a habit of praying with other women. Paul and his companions deliberately went out to the river expecting to find a place of prayer, and there they found women gathered, including Lydia. "More than likely Lydia is well-to-do as a seller of purple, a luxury good associated with wealth throughout Mediterranean culture for over a thousand years. . . . Well-to-do women sometimes became patrons, or sponsors, of pagan religious associations; those attracted to Judaism helped support Jewish causes" (Craig S. Keener, *The IVP Bible Background Commentary: New Testament* [Downers Grove, Ill.: InterVarsity Press, 1993], pp. 368-69).

Question 5. "Paul and his companions may have been staying at an inn till the sabbath, but Lydia immediately offers the proper Jewish hospitality and invites the apostles into her home, thus serving as a patron of their work" (Keener, p. 369). The Greek word translated "persuaded" indicates that Lydia did more than make a mild suggestion. She practically compelled the apostles to stay at her home. The only other time this Greek word appears in the New Testament is in Luke 24:29, where the two disciples on the road to Emmaus urge the risen Christ to stay with them.

Question 8. It was one thing for Lydia to take in the visiting party when they first arrived in Philippi. It was another thing for her to accept them back after their night in jail. When they came back to Lydia's house, they didn't just grab their luggage and leave; she let them stay long enough to meet with other believers and encourage them. Lydia had a healthy disregard for other people's opinions of her hospitality.

Question 9. Lydia risked her own personal safety; she could not know for sure who these men were. She risked her possessions; they could have been thieves. She risked her reputation, both personal and business; neighbors might not understand her taking in this group of unknown men, and the city would raise eyebrows at her taking them back after they had been arrested, beaten and jailed overnight.

Questions 10-11. Group members may answer in general terms, but encourage them to also answer out of specific personal experience.

Study 5. Give Us Ten Days: Imaginative Problem-Solving. Daniel 1:1-21.

Purpose: To open our minds to God's alternatives for solving seemingly impossible problems.

Questions 3-4. "Daniel arrived in Babylon in 605 [B.C.] . . . . Good looks and natural ability ensured a place for him and his friends among those selected for special training. But the Babylonians did not observe Jewish rules on clean and unclean food (Leviticus 11), nor did they drain away the blood when they slaughtered animals

(Leviticus 17:10ff.). Young as they were, Daniel and his friends were determined not to compromise their religion" (David Alexander and Pat Alexander, eds., *Eerdmans' Handbook to the Bible* [Grand Rapids, Mich.: Eerdmans, 1973], p. 430).

Question 5. The official's problem is that of a lot of middle-management people. In their hearts they want to play fair with the people below them on the ladder, but they need to protect themselves from the appearance of failure because they're afraid of the repercussions from above.

Question 6. If you are in a group, no one should feel obligated to voice a problem. These "impossible" problems are often hard to talk about and even inappropriate to talk about in a group. Their privacy is one factor which makes them so difficult. Try to be sure everyone has at least one such problem in mind. If a person has no current situation like this, suggest thinking of one in the past. Later in the study it would be interesting to hear how those past situations turned out.

Question 7. Daniel found a way to give the chief official what he needed while protecting his own conscience and the consciences of his three friends. In this attractive scenario everyone would be a winner. The element of conflict in the situation was defused because no one would lose.

Question 8. Going with the flow can be healthy if it means trusting the Lord and letting go of the problem. However, it may mean an unhealthy passivity which has given up on the Lord having any solution.

Study 6. Never Too Late: Taking Initiative. Ruth 2:1-12.
Purpose: To look toward the future and originate new possibilities with God's help.

Question 1. Look over previous studies to pick out ways that Jeannie has initiated solutions to her problems. Suggestions: Study 1—She stopped moping about her surroundings and took steps to make her home more attractive. Study 2—She took an interest in finding out what was troubling Will. Study 3—She gave Ann a personally created gift and offered to teach a skill. Study 4—She opened her home for ministry. Study 5—She suggested an alternative plan for the training. Study 6—She suggested a way for Ann to take responsibility and take care of her own needs.

Question 3. Gleaning was "the practice of gathering or picking up what was left in the field after reaping. It also applied to grapes left under the vine or olives in the orchard. Technically, 'gleaning' also applied to reaping what was left standing in the corners of the field. Hebrew law prohibited an owner from cleaning up his own field, vineyard, or orchard, so that there would be provision for the poor, the orphan, the widow, and the alien resident" (H. N. Richardson, "Gleaning," in *Interpreter's Dictionary*, vol. 2, p. 401). Ruth fell into all of those categories.

Question 5. God provided the relative of Naomi who had the means to help them. He led Ruth to Boaz's field, then led Boaz there in time to notice her. He softened Boaz's heart toward Ruth so that he was generous to her.

Question 7. Christians deal constantly with the issue of how much we should do ourselves and how much we should stand back and let the Lord do for us. Ruth is a great example of God and a believer working together. We could say that God placed Ruth in the right field, but he did not pick her up bodily and transport her there; she had to decide to go, walk to the field, start gleaning and keep gleaning when she wanted to quit.

Question 9. This question is related to question 8 in study 5 concerning Daniel's imaginative solution to the problem of defiling himself with the Babylonians' food. Do we say, "I'll wait and see what God does" in faith and hope, or do we say it in gloomy resignation? It will be helpful for group members to hear each other's answers as to how they have made the distinction.

InterVarsity Press Bible Studies by Sandy Larsen

Women of Character Bible Studies
A Woman of Creativity
A Woman of Grace

LifeGuide® Bible Studies
(with Dale Larsen)
Faith
Hosea

Teamwork Discipleship Guides (with Dale Larsen)
Starting with Christ
Maturing in Christ